Facing Mortality

Dreams & Other Significant Things

Facing Mortality

Dreams & Other Significant Things

THERESA SNEED

Dedication

Lovingly dedicated to those who have been a part of my life and gone home before me.

Acknowledgments

Many thanks to Nanette O'Neal who read this short work with a keen eye for content and grammar.

Author Theresa Sneed
www.theresasneed.com

Dear Reader,

I hope you enjoy reading *Facing Mortality: Dreams & other Significant Things*. If you loved this book, please consider leaving a good review everywhere. Your kind words might be the reason that someone else decides to read my books, and for that, I thank you in advance. ☺

Stay connected with new releases and free e book offers by signing up at my website at www.theresasneed.com.

- Author, Theresa Sneed

Other Titles by Theresa Sneed

No Angel Series
Angel with an Attitude
Earthbound Angel
Destiny's Angel
Earth Angel
Harold Angel Sing

Sons of Elderberry Series
Elias of Elderberry
The Wood Fairies of Estraelia
Missing Medallion

Escape Series
Escape
You Can't Hide
Find Her Keep Her

Salem Witch Haunt series
Salem Witch Haunt
Return to Salem
Salem Bewitched

Brown Nose Bear

Facing Mortality
Dreams & Other Significant Things

So, You Want to Write
A Guide to Writing Your First Book

Prologue

par·a·nor·mal
adj.

Beyond the range of normal experience or scientific explanation.

I was nine years old when I had my first experience with the paranormal, and it was definitely beyond the range of normal experience or scientific explanation.

One

Man in White
Dairy Farm, Dover-Foxcroft, Maine, USA
Circa 1966-67
Age: 9 or 10

Though it was many years ago, I vividly remember the bedroom I shared with my older sister JoAnn. It was the only living space upstairs. Its east and west walls were short and connected to sloping walls up to a flat ceiling—giving it the appearance of a large coffin. Though it was small, it was big enough for our twin beds which straddled a heat register in the middle of the floor. The only source of heat in the bitterly cold Maine winters, the register was a focal point in our room. A square box with an iron scroll grille on the top and the bottom, the top of the grille was in the floor of our bedroom and the bottom was in the ceiling of the room beneath us.

At some point we discovered that the top could be removed, and we could fit one of our sneaky heads down into it, and though upside down, could watch whatever TV program our parents had sent us to bed early not to see. I often wonder what fear would have gripped me if Daddy had looked up to see my conniving eyes looking down.

The bedroom had one window that looked out over the meadow and woods, and it had three doors. One led down an enclosed stairwell to the kitchen, another was a short door to a small cubby, and the third opened into the attic, which was beside the bedroom. JoAnn slept in the bed closest to the window. My bed was by the attic door. The door that led downstairs to the kitchen was at the foot of our beds.

The attic held a secret of mine, as it became the burial place of a small litter of premature kittens, which my tiny hands lovingly laid to rest amongst the soft, rock wool insulation under its worn boards. My mother would have been horrified, but I never told anyone, not even JoAnn. We had forty-two cats at one time on the farm, and though we weren't allowed to have any cats in the house, with the attic that close, JoAnn and I often broke that rule. The attic was one of the many areas the cats roamed as the old farmhouse attic had access to it from the attached sheds.

One evening, JoAnn had stayed late at a friend's house and after returning, fell asleep downstairs on one of the two couches in the living room. I awoke during the night and went downstairs for a drink of water. I left the upstairs door open. As I ascended the stairs, I saw a man, all arrayed in white, sitting on JoAnn's bed facing mine. He was white from the top of his head down to his feet—his face, hair, and hands, *every part of him* was white.

I am a logical person, and even at a young age, I looked for answers—reasons for this strange phenomenon. I did not turn and run but quickly surmised the situation. I looked to the register to see if any light from it could be causing the image I saw. I checked the window and the attic door for any signs of light. There wasn't any, and yet the being remained, eyes fixed on me. He did not do or say anything, I suppose he waited for my reaction to him. He presented no danger to me, nor reason to fear him, but I did. I'm convinced that a staunch

Baptist upbringing entrenched in unnatural fear gripped my young heart, of which I sorely regret. I inched my way over to my bed and snatched a pillow. Hurrying downstairs to the second couch, our family dog by my side, I didn't sleep, but prayed for protection for the rest of the night.

Who was that being, and what was his purpose? Did he have a message for me or perhaps a request? Dare I imagine I held some importance to him, or was he merely resting before continuing his journey?

Unlike other spirits I would later see and compare him to, he stands alone in uniqueness—no other spirit was completely white. I do know, as anyone would, that he was not of this world, at that moment at least. Perhaps he was an ancestor returning to stir my heart towards spiritual matters, or an angel of God, or maybe even the Savior Himself. It doesn't matter who he was. At a young age, I got the message—there is more to life than meets the eye.

Life appears to be swathed in mystery—the mystery of the purpose of life and its inevitable, certain passing, or death. What I saw at that moment was not hearsay, the hope of another person, or merely the faith of one who believes, but it was *knowledge*. What I was privileged to witness is *proof* that another part of life exists. Death is not the final curtain.

Two

Angelic Chorus
Dairy Farm, Dover-Foxcroft, Maine
Circa 1967-8
Age: 10 or 11

I do not remember much about this, but I do remember it happening. I share this experience with my sister JoAnn. I don't remember the day or year, or whether it was spring or summer, or night or day, but I do remember the music we heard in our upstairs bedroom. Music that came from nowhere, for we searched everywhere for its source. Beautiful, peaceful angelic choruses floating gently through our room.

Three

Near Death . . . *A Choice of Life*
BYU Provo, Utah, USA
1977
Age: 19

It was the winter semester at BYU Provo. After transferring from USC following the fall semester there, I had for many reasons concluded that life was everlastingly too hard. I was deeply saddened by the events in the world around me and by the choices of friends and loved ones. As a freshman 3,000 miles from home who hadn't been home for five months, I was terribly homesick too.

Along with that, I was also a little depressed due to feeling so alone at BYU. I had joined the church at USC, transferred to BYU, and knew very few people. Because I worked the nightshift fulltime, I didn't get to socialize at all. The two students who transferred from USC to BYU with me had become great friends, and I felt like more of a bother to them, not a friend. One had a car and a bank account her father kept up for her. She really liked the other girl and took her everywhere. They never asked me to go with them. I didn't have a car, and from January to April walked two to three miles each wintery night to work, and then walked home in the morning. I barely made enough money to pay for my rent at the Riviera Apartments and for my own food. I had classes at 10:00 am and sometimes concerts in the evening, as I played the String Bass in the BYU Symphony Orchestra. I remember a couple of times not going to bed at all but going from work—to school—to play in a concert—and then back to work.

I guess I had had enough, and one evening deep in thought, I unwittingly willed myself to go *home*. It wasn't anything I was attempting to do, it just happened. I lay on my bed at the apartment and simply asked to come home, back to my Father in heaven, exercising the faith that I had. The faith and the will I had was in conjunction with the spirit. I felt very close to the Lord. A swirling sensation started from my feet and moved up through my body, and I felt like my spirit was leaving my body. It frightened me, so I stopped it.

I write about it because it is such a fascinating experience. The faith, the answer, the reprieve—the story of my mortal life continues as such—always being saved from myself.

Four

First Impressions
Cincinnati, Ohio, USA
1977
Age: 20

Do you believe in love at first sight? I believe in love *before* first sight.

After I finished my freshman year at USC and BYU, I returned home for the summer. I rode a Greyhound bus for four days from Provo, Utah, to, I think, Dexter Maine. I remember it wasn't Dover. I remember, because I was so excited to get home, but when I finally got to the bus depot, there was no one there to pick me up. I called a friend, she came, end of sad story. I wasn't home too long before the youthful need to be out on my own enticed me to purchase a plane ticket to visit my sister JoAnn, in Cincinnati, Ohio.

I met a couple of girls who became my friends in Ohio, Karen Adams and Holly Wilson. We decided to have a talent show, and I went to see the stake president, President Banks to see if we could. He said, yes, and gave us a list of young adult representatives in the stake to call for help. Bill's name was on the list. I called him, and he came to the first meeting at the Norwood Stake Center in Norwood, Ohio.

When I walked into the auditorium, I saw Bill sitting cross-legged on the stage. He was tapping a hammer rhythmically between his legs. There wasn't anything so dramatic about him to cause me to feel the way that I did, but when I saw him, I had the sudden urge to passionately kiss him. Now, you have to know me to know how out of character that is for me. I was actually taken aback by my unexpected desire and felt embarrassed at my thought.

Where did that feeling come from? Why was I immediately attracted to a man that I had never seen before? And why a kiss? Why not just a, "I wonder who he is? He's cute!" or "I'd like to meet him." But a kiss? A kiss is a form of greeting you share with someone with whom you are already familiar and intimate with. I think the greater part of me (my spirit) recognized the greater part of Bill (his spirit) from our relationship before this mortal experience. Kind of like how John felt when he leapt for joy in Martha's womb when Martha and Mary met, who was pregnant with his cousin, Jesus—spirit recognizing spirit.

I'm convinced that the great love I have for Bill had its beginnings in another setting.

The night of the talent show.

Five

Unexpected Visitors
Sneed Residence, Batavia Ohio, USA
Late 1978 or early 1979
Age: 21

I was three months pregnant with our oldest son Jason, when I pulled a string of muscles in my back lifting a small TV. The doctor told me to stay in bed for two weeks while it healed. We left our small apartment in Batavia and stayed at Bill's parent's home on the other side of town. I remember the loving way that Bill's mother, Shirley, took care of me. One day she peeled a pink grapefruit, broke it into wedges, and sprinkled it with sugar. I had never had pink grapefruit prepared like that before, but more especially had not been pampered since I was a child years ago by my own mother.

We stayed in Bill's brother, Lorin's room. It was a small bedroom, but we managed to put a TV in the corner, and our three-year old daughter Mandee's sleeping bag on the floor beside us. There was a window across from the bed and a dresser against the same wall the headboard rested against. The bed was alongside the wall opposite the window. I slept on the outside of the bed for easier access both in and out of bed.

I awoke one night to find two men dressed in white standing by my bed. They were not frightening in the least. In fact, it seemed quite natural and not out of the ordinary to see them. The one on the left reached his hand out to me, and said, "It's time to go." I began to sit up and reached my hand out to his, but looked back at my husband and said, "No. I want to stay with Bill." I do not remember anything past that. I must have simply cuddled next to Bill and gone back to sleep.

Was it a dream? If anything had been out of place in that room, I may have wondered so, but there wasn't. The room was exactly the way it was when I went to sleep that night. I noted that the TV was in the corner, the dresser to my right, Bill on the other side of me, and Mandee sleeping soundly on the floor. There just happened to be two men, dressed in white, standing there too.

Was it my time to go? Apparently not, but maybe so. Did I have a choice? Perhaps. Was it the same choice that I had at BYU? I think so. And yet, a greater message is woven in the fibers of this experience. *I turned to Bill and chose him.*

Six

Jason's Spirit
Batavia, Ohio, USA
August 1978

Some will argue that a baby has not life until a certain time has elapsed in its fetal development. I know differently. I felt my son's spirit enter the body Bill and I had created for him shortly after conception. Bill was in the next room, and I sat thoughtfully on the bed. A swirling sensation, similar to the one I experienced at BYU, only in the reverse direction, began from my head and came down through my body to my mid torso. I didn't know what it was then but made the connection a couple months later when I found out I was pregnant. I have never felt that with any of my other children, only Jason. Who art thou, Jason to have a spirit so strong and so determined? – a spirit with a great purpose, yet to be defined.

Seven

Young Spirits
Dover-Foxcroft, Maine, USA
Phoenix, Arizona, USA
Mesa, Arizona, USA
1988 - February 14, 2002

The first time I saw her was in Dover-Foxcroft, Maine. She was wearing a knee length dress and had long hair. She looked directly at me, and then turned around and passed though the upstairs hallway in front of me—not up or down the hallway, but through the walls on either side.

The second time I saw this young spirit was in Phoenix, AZ, on 29th Ave and Union Hills. It was the same thing, only the hallway was on the ground floor. I stepped into the hallway and saw her pass through the walls again.

The third time was rather interesting. Four of our closest friends, the Loves and the Gentrys, and Bill and I, performed forty temple sealings in the Mesa Temple of the Church of Jesus Christ of Latter-day Saints. It happened to fall on Valentine's Day—which was kind of sweet. We were in a small sealing room that had a narrow stairwell leading up to it. It was hot that day. I can't recall if there had been a problem with the air conditioning or not, but the room was stuffy. They told us they were going to leave the door open a bit to let the air circulate, as they had had a patron faint earlier.

We took turns in the various sealings, and when it wasn't

my turn, I occasionally found my gaze wandering to the partially opened door. I saw a group of women walk past the door, and only saw the hems of their long white dresses, and then I saw a young girl, of about ten years or so pass by. The curious thing is that she later passed by going back the way she came, and then she passed by the door again. There was a young boy—a little taller than she was, with her one of those times. I also observed that I could see temple workers talking to each other at the foot of the stairs and noted that I could only see the top part of them, as the stairs obstructed a full-length view.

After the sealings, I lingered for a while, pondering the eternal nature of a temple sealing. When I went to leave the room, I was absolutely surprised. There wasn't a hallway on the top of the stairwell where I had seen the hems of the group of women pass by as well as the young girl and boy. There was only the enclosed stairwell going down to the lower floor.

I immediately went to see the person in charge of sealings and inquired if there had been any children sealed to their parents that afternoon. He said no, but earlier that morning they had had a Hispanic couple with children sealed. Because I could compare the women's hems and the full-length view of the two children passing by the room with the temple workers at the bottom of the stairs that I could only see from the waist up, I concluded that these indeed had been spirits who had witnessed their own sealings and were most definitely family members of mine.

Still, I sealed no children to their parents that day. Who were they, and what message were they trying to send to me?

I haven't seen her since, perhaps someone else heeded her call, but I suspect that one day, she'd going to ask me why I didn't jump on it right away and search for her, so I guess, I better do it, just in case she's still waiting. For those of you who are not familiar with temples and their purpose, visit lds.org/temples/purpose.

Eight

Who Drove the Car?
On route from Batavia, Ohio, USA to Dover-
Foxcroft, Maine, USA
June 1980

The news of my mother's death was sudden and devastating. We had spent the day at Bill's parent's home in Batavia, Ohio, picking berries from their cherry tree in the front yard. My brother Jeff had not been able to reach me at our home and had later decided to try Bill's parent's number. I answered the phone and was excited to hear my younger brother's familiar voice. I remember even joking with him about beating him at monopoly, a family favorite in our youth. He didn't laugh but asked to speak to Bill. I thought it odd, but handed the phone to Bill, only to see his face drop, and hear him say, "Oh, no!"

It was already evening in Ohio, and we lived a good forty-minute drive from his parent's home. JoAnn had moved to South Carolina and was in anguish, because she had no way to get to Maine. I approached Bill's dad, and he loaned her the money for the ticket, but we had to drive one and a half hours just to get to the airport to pay for the ticket and have it transferred to South Carolina for her. By the time we purchased the ticket, drove back to our home—another two hours—and packed, it was close to midnight.

We still left that evening and began a twenty-four-hour nonstop drive to Maine. I barely could keep my eyes open and really don't remember much of the drive. When it was my turn to drive, I remember waking up from time to time *while I was driving.* I was absolutely humbled to discover that Bill had the exact same experience as I. We were not driving that night—someone else was.

Nine

Mandee's Gift
Dover-Foxcroft, Maine, USA
November 6, 1990

I recorded this in my journal years ago.

Last night something really special happened to Mandee. She was chosen to experience a spiritual manifestation. We were taking turns reading chapter eight in A Witness and Warning. We were on the last page, and Mandee was reading a quote from Mormon to his son Moroni. (Moroni 9:25-26)

"My son, be faithful in Christ, and may not the things which I have written grieve thee, to weigh thee down unto death; but may Christ lift thee up, and may his sufferings and death, and the showing his body unto our fathers, and his mercy and long suffering, and the hope of his glory and of eternal life, rest in your mind forever.

And may the grace of God the Father, whose throne is high in the heavens, and our Lord Jesus Christ, who sitteth on the right hand of his power, until all things shall become subject unto him, be, and abide with you forever."

Partway through these scriptures she looked up at me, smiled sweetly, and then said, "Oh, you know this scripture."

I can't remember what my response was. She read a few more lines then stopped again and said, "You have this memorized." I was a little bewildered as to why she said something like that twice to me, so I asked her what she meant. She said, "You're reciting this, so you must have it memorized."

I wasn't saying a thing while she was reading, and I told her so. She asked if Jason had been, and he wasn't either. Bill was not home yet, and not expected home until after their bedtime. Then Mandee said, "I thought you were whispering what I was reading—the same scripture."

I wasn't.

I believe that she was privileged to bridge the veil for a brief moment and have a wonderful, faith-promoting spiritual experience. She began reading again and kept looking up in bewilderment because she could still hear someone reciting that scripture to her.

Don't forget this, my sweet, chosen daughter!

The veil between heaven and earth is very thin, and we have but to listen to discover some of its hidden messages.

Ten

Brotherly Love
Dover-Foxcroft, Maine, USA
Batavia Ohio, USA
Chicago Temple, Chicago, Illinois, USA
1990-91

My brother Donnie and I are "Irish twins." He was only ten months and eight days older than me, and for thirty-seven days each year, we shared the same age. Donnie was a prankster. Once he dared me to drink a gallon of water for a dollar. We went together to the water spigot in the barn. Donnie watched with an almost devilish look in his eye, as I filled the gallon jar, and slowly, with great agony, drank every last drop. His intent had always been to punch me in the stomach once I was full, so that's what he did. I was not completely surprised, it wasn't out of his character then. I was quite sick though. Mom told him to pay me the dollar, though I don't think he ever did.

We were living in Gilbert, Arizona, and had just returned home from playing miniature golf, when I got the call. Donnie had had an argument with his girlfriend and left her house in Greenfield, Maine, with three times the level of alcohol in his blood. He ran his vehicle into the back of a logging truck and died that night in June.

Donnie was very intelligent. He graduated from Maine Maritime Academy, had traveled the world, and was well read. In his adult years, he spent a lot of his downtime between shipping out at my house. We had many in depth conversations. Unfortunately, because I lived 3000 miles away, I arrived one day too late for his funeral, and had a strange casket-side service with the Nazarene minister in our small town. I can still see the twisted look on his face when I thanked him for quoting one of my favorite scriptures about the Savior. He didn't have much faith in my choice of faiths.

Shortly after Donnie's death, we moved to Maine for the first time in our marriage. We remained there for three years, until the death of my father, then decided to move back to Arizona. Because we were short on money, we determined that working in Bill's father's family business for a few months in Ohio would help us to move on to Arizona.

About a year before we moved to Ohio, I had an incredible dream about Donnie. In my dream, I opened a door and entered a pristine waiting room. Donnie entered through a door on the other side of the room. He was radiant. The color of his face, the blue of his eyes, the white of his teeth were like colors I had never seen before, far greater augmented and brighter than any earthly hues. He called me by my name, and we embraced. The next morning, I couldn't remember anything else, because I was not meant to. But when I awoke I had one of those smiles plastered on my face that was so intense that it hurt. Was it a dream? I don't think so. The colors were nothing I had ever experienced here in mortality. And the joy I had upon awakening needs no confirmation nor explanation.

After we had been in Ohio for about a year, Bill's parents' ward sent several of their youth ahead of the adults to the

Chicago Temple to do baptisms for the dead. Our son and our daughter went with them. After they left, and had already arrived at the temple, I realized that our son Jason could do Donnie's baptism, so I called the temple and requested that he be allowed to do my brother's work. Proper protocol was to send a family group sheet along, and I hadn't. Someone in the Chicago Temple decided to call Salt Lake, which surprised and delighted me, and Jason got special permission from Salt Lake to perform Donnie's baptism.

One of the sisters in the ward, Debbie Glutz, had witnessed it. She later told me that Jason had already performed his fifteen baptisms and had redressed, but they had him change back into baptismal clothing again and participate in Donnie's baptism. She said it was very spiritual. Jason had known Donnie all of his young life. The next day, we arrived to do the rest of the ordinances, and a particularly interesting thing happened.

In a special location of the temple—a place where no one speaks out loud, my brother Donnie, more than three years deceased, audibly called me by name.

He was there! He was there while his temple work was being done. I recognized his voice immediately. It was a special gift to me—to know that he was there. But, my dead brother speaks to me, and what was my first reaction?

Shh! You're not supposed to talk here!

He's dead, manifesting himself to me, and I'm concerned about him talking out loud. So me. But my second reaction was one of complete elation. I turned to look for him, but saw nothing, but I know it was him. It was his distinctive voice. I'm sure I was kept from seeing him because I would have literally squealed with delight!

How can I ever question the reality of things not seen? The Lord has blessed me beyond measure with many out-of-the-ordinary personal experiences that testify to life beyond this life. I know, without a doubt, for I witnessed it, that my brother Donnie was there that day and continues to work hard on the other side of the veil in behalf of me, our siblings, and our families, after all, he still owes me a dollar.

Donald Malcom Small, Jr.
"Donnie"
Born: May 20, 1956
Died: June 6, 1988

Eleven

Death Dreams: Part I
Batavia, Ohio, USA
1999

What are dreams? Are they the imaginations of the heart or the soul at play without imposed limitations to restrict it? Do they have meaning, messages from beyond? And what of unexplained phenomena, has it a purpose? I think, yes.

2000 was a difficult year for me. We had been living in Pennsylvania for two years and decided to move back to Ohio to build our dream home. Bill's parents were going to help us by giving us an acre of wooded land and by allowing us to live with them while we prepared to build. I spent hours of back-breaking work pulling out humungous briar bushes and vines that intertwined the entire forest bed then wickedly crept up the tall trees wrapping themselves around every branch and leaf on the property. Bill spent all his time after work cutting and burning trees and brush to clear our land.

Kathy, an old friend of Bill's family, took me aside and cautioned, "I hope this will really become yours." I shook it off, determined to make the dream come true. I was destined for a hard fall.

I really can't blame it on Bill's mother, Shirley, though at the time, she did things that hurt and depressed me. Kathy, and another friend, told me that she was spreading unkind rumors about my "laziness" around church.

I had become quite depressed, and only after the kids were off to school, and all of my duties in her house were finished, did I choose to lay on my bed immersed in my depression. I had nowhere to go. I didn't have any good friends at church or in the community. I have never felt that unwanted and unneeded in my life.

So, I thought that a trip to Maine would lift my spirits. I could unload on my sisters and my brother for the first time in my adult life—really let them know how miserable I was and seek their advice and comfort. That's not what I found in Maine.

Bill couldn't take the time off, so I drove to Maine with our four youngest children by myself. That part went surprisingly smoothly. The mess I dropped in on at the family campout at Sebec Lake changed my life, for the worst at first, and then for the better.

I remember pitching our tent with the help of my young boys in the pouring rain, but it was so beautiful at the wooded edge of the lake, and I was home, so it didn't matter. After the tent was up, I went to the next campsite to visit with my sister JoAnn.

The very first words out of her mouth were harsh and painful, though I chose not to recall them. I do remember, without much effort, that they had something to do with my children, and something more to do with twenty years of pent-up frustration from all my siblings and siblings-in-law of my holier-than-thou attitude.

They were right. But I needed their love, especially at that delicate moment in my life. However, instead of reacting in a healthy way, I gave it right back. I remember passing my sister Sue on the hill after fighting with JoAnn and anticipating her support for "poor me", but her reaction surprised and dismayed me.

I packed my tent and left, crying all the way to a friend's house. JoAnn called immediately. We talked, yelled, talked, and yelled. I left Maine without seeing them again and headed back to Ohio, far more depressed than when I had left.

I allowed myself to get caught up in a self-righteous pity party back in Ohio. I guess I may have had a bit of pent-up frustration for those twenty years of being treated differently by them too. Nonetheless, we got entangled in family internet mud-slinging, which ended with bitter feelings between my younger sister Sue and me, even though the original fight was between JoAnn and me.

JoAnn came out of her way to see me in Ohio a few months later. We talked, really talked, and I came to truly understand her perspective. It took Suzie and me much longer to mend our differences, but before that was to happen, I guess God knew I would need help from beyond the veil to change my attitude.

It was during that time that I had my first death dream, and though it had little to do with altering my attitude, it was nonetheless a fascinating dream and laid the foundation for the dreams to come.

I dreamt that I had died. Even in my dream, I could not remember how I had died, but I knew that I was recently dead. In my dream, my deceased family came to see me. There was a large group of them. My brother Donnie was not there, but I was told that he would come to see me as soon as he was finished with something that he was doing.

In the next part of my dream, I was in a dormitory room with a woman named Linda, who was also recently dead. She was tall and had short blond hair. She was not familiar to me. We gathered our stuff together to leave the dormitory. We walked toward a large building where we, and other recently deceased spirits, were going to attend an important meeting.

I remember seeing the building off in the distance and green grass to the right of the sidewalk. We got there about halfway when we remembered we had left something in the dormitory. It was an iron of sorts. I can't explain it because I don't understand it. It was very unusual in a futuristic sort of way. How difficult it is for any time-trapped mortal to explain an object of eternity.

We paused for a moment as we discussed going back to get the iron. I did not want to go, but Linda did. I watched her walk back towards the dormitory. I felt a little guilty, so I started to follow her, but stopped, as I thought, "Wait! I'm dead! Why am I walking?" So, I simply thought about where I wanted to go and instantly was there.

It must have been a dream, because here I am today, but what a fascinating dream it was! To dream so clearly of the moments following death, greeting my family, anticipating seeing my brother Donnie as soon as he was able, having a recently dead roommate, preparing to go to an important meeting, and transporting myself back to the dormitory rather than using any snail-pace mortal means.

What great fun! What a great adventure this mortal life has been—for a short moment in time—I am limited in my eternal, god-like abilities in order to glean as much as possible from this human-like experience. We are all gods in embryo, not unlike our creator, but created in His literal image.

Twelve

Death Dreams: Part II
Gilbert, Arizona, USA
June or July 2000

Kathy had been right—having our dream home in Ohio was not meant to be. Though I can now look back and recognize my part in the rocky relationship that I had with Bill's mother, we ended up leaving Ohio to search for a different home. We moved back to Arizona, where I was about to embark on a life changing journey.

Our youngest child Saralynn would enter first grade soon, and as I had always planned, I would find a fulltime job. I checked out several possibilities, from working in a local deli, to working with the elderly in their homes. Then one evening, Bill showed me an ad in the newspaper for an airline ticket salesperson. Free airfare was really attractive to me, so I applied.

As an older woman, entering the work force was intimidating. I sat in a large room with about a hundred, mostly younger, people. They called us in one at a time to be interviewed, and I was elated to have been one of the thirty chosen. They gave me a small booklet to memorize about their airplanes and the abbreviations of their many destinations. I made a three-inch stack of flash cards, and hounded anyone who dare come near, to quiz me. I had two weeks to memorize it with 80% proficiency, or I would be terminated. I was confident I'd get 100%.

The day of the test arrived. I awoke early, got the kids up and dressed, cleaned the house, and arrived twenty minutes early for the test. I approached the counter and asked where I was to go. He looked down at his schedule, then up at me, and then he said, "You were supposed to be here four hours ago."

It was then I remembered that the test was supposed to be in the morning, and that the training would be in the afternoons. I'd have to wait a whole month to take the test.

On the way home, I was in an amused daze. Try as I might to feel disappointed, I couldn't. How could I have memorized an entire booklet and forgotten a simple time?

Now I was free to go to the American Night Writers Summer Retreat, where I met up with a dear friend, Betsy Love, whom I hadn't seen for years. She worked as a theater teacher in a charter school in Mesa. She encouraged me to apply there. I had taken several education courses but did not have my degree. I did not believe that I could work as a teacher, but the idea of being a teacher's aide appealed to me.

After the retreat, I applied as an aide in my neighborhood elementary school. I had an appointment to meet with the principal later that week. The day before the appointment, I went with Bill to his office and just happened to glance over and see a sign on a building that said, Sequoia School. I wondered if it was Betsy's school. Bill's office was right around the corner from the school, so after Bill went in his office, I went back to check it out.

It was Betsy's school. I asked for an application, and as if prompted to act differently, instead of applying as a teacher's aide, I applied for the elementary music teacher position. I wrote down all of my musical and educational experiences and then left.

Betsy came by my house the next day all excited because the principal wanted to interview me. She drove me to Sequoia. I was interviewed by Ron Palmer, whom along with Betsy, I will forever be grateful for believing in me. They hired me the next day as a fulltime music teacher. I loved my job!

I was meant to be a music teacher, not an airline ticket salesperson. I didn't know it at the time, but someone else did. I never would have forgotten something as simple as the time a test was at, but someone else caused me to forget it, as they gently guided me toward my destiny.

It was around that time that I had my second death dream. The dream lasted the entire night. I dreamt that a small group of spirits were trying to reach me. They were Native American Indians. I purposely evaded them from dream to dream. They came to *each dream* I had that evening, all night long. I wasn't afraid of them, even though I knew that they were spirits. It was as if I knew what they wanted but didn't want to comply. Towards the morning, I could evade them no longer and finally allowed them to speak to me. They wanted me to return with them to the spirit world. They wanted me to sing with them in some kind of a concert. I chose not to go.

Interesting, huh? And yet, the very next night, I had an even more fascinating death dream, though it was not a dream at all.

Thirteen

Death Dreams: Part III
Gilbert, Arizona, USA
June or July 2000

In the middle of the night, I awoke and found my deceased father standing across from me, at the foot of my bed. Bill was sleeping in between us. My dad called me by my nickname, Terri. It was wonderful to hear his voice! The mortal voices of deceased loved ones are hard for me to pull from memory, but when they speak, I recognize them immediately. Daddy didn't say anything else, but I knew what he wanted. He wanted me to return with him.

I said, "I will be obedient," but then began to cry as my eyes rested on Bill. I said, "I love you," to Bill three times, as I lay back down. I heard a soft rumbling sound, and I felt a gentle swirling sensation grow in intensity and surround my body— similar to the experience at BYU. I instinctively knew that if I did nothing, my spirit would leave my body, so I stopped it.

Instantly, Daddy was gone, and I was *not asleep*. I had nothing to wake up from, no pulling myself out from any sort of dream state or dreamy awakening. I was not sleeping, so did not need to awake. I was simply there, alone with Bill sleeping by my side.

What does one do, when in an instant a pretty incredible

experience ends, and you are left to ponder its meaning? Does one simply go back to sleep? Oh, no, no, no, no.

I immediately got out of bed and on my knees. I told my Heavenly Father that I would be obedient, if indeed he wanted me to come home that evening, then I would go, but, if I could choose, then I choose to stay *with Bill.*

Then I sat down and wrote the whole experience out and a message to each one of my children—just in case. It's handwritten on a piece of yellow cardstock paper.

I am not afraid of death. It holds little mystery but all wonder to me. I imagine when I do leave this existence, it will be quite like the dreams I've had—*only better.* However, if Bill should leave mortality before me, and then come for me— there is nothing on this earth that would keep me from leaping into his arms. Until then, I'd like to stay just a little longer, and try a little harder, to be a little better. And I'll keep asking as long as it doesn't interfere with the Lord's will for me.

Fourteen

Message from Beyond: Part I
Early 2004

As mentioned earlier, I had been quite frustrated with my younger sister Sue and her attitude toward me. There's no need to write about it, only to say that during a long period of time, I would only consider my perspective, and my self-pitying suffering, not hers. The dreams that I had, especially this one early in 2004, helped me to see things differently.

I dreamt about my deceased parents. I rarely dream about them and always love it when I do—except for this time. They were not happy with me. Dad was so upset that he wouldn't even come into the house. Mom and I were standing in their old bedroom, which today has been remodeled into a kitchen by my brother Jeff. I was facing her bureau, and the bed was behind and to the right of me. Mom was facing me. She wouldn't look at me but gestured to small piles of stuff strewn around the room. She simply said, "Clean up this mess."

Immediately, I was upstairs in my old bedroom. Outside, level with my two-story window, there was a pile of, um, *cow manure* stacked from the ground up. On the top of the manure there was a single plant with a few small, white flowers. Later, I mused at the thought of my dad refusing to come into the house so he could prepare this special message for me. I'll bet he knew I would eventually get it—to clean up my own pile of ----. Thanks, Dad, and by the way, the flowers were a nice touch. I never needed to be reminded that I loved Sue, but I did need to be reminded that I had a part in our problem.

Fifteen

This dream is related to the previous one. I had this dream about six months later.

I dreamt that I was in Sue and our youngest sister Shari's old bedroom. Mom, who had passed away twenty-four years earlier, was there with me and this time she was pleased. The room had been cleaned out and had been prepared to paint. There were smooth drywall patches on several holes in the walls. Then I looked, and the room was nearly painted. I was holding a paint brush. Mom smiled and said, "You forgot a place." She pointed to a small patch about three inches in diameter. I wanted her to see that there was a larger spot, about two feet long over the threshold, so I pointed it out to her. She was disappointed when she saw it.

What does that dream mean? Was it significant that there was a large unfinished area over the threshold, the entrance to Sue and Shari's old room? —or that someone had prepped the room for me to paint? Even though the threshold was mended with smooth, clean patches and ready to paint, it was above my reach, so maybe it was someone else's turn to paint.

Evidently so, because after five long years of not speaking to each other, Sue and I repaired our relationship, and today I count her as a dear sister and friend. Still, I wonder who intervened and fixed that threshold—*someone* helped mend both our hearts.

Sixteen

Facing Mortality
Banner Baywood Heart Hospital
Mesa, Arizona, USA
April 29, 2008

I didn't know if I would live, or if I would die. A critical case of deep-vein thrombosis and pulmonary embolism found me in a hospital bed wondering what God's will was for me.

From my bed, I wrote, ". . . it doesn't matter, because there is nothing greater than His will. Should I die this instant, life for me will continue on in a different realm. However, let me explain that that different realm is not different at all.

Mortality is actually the different realm.

Our *true reality* is where we came from before we were born into mortality and where we will return after we leave mortality—back to our true home. I have spent a lot of time pondering the meaning of these two scriptures:

For a thousand years in thy sight are but yesterday when it is past, and as a watch in the night. Psalm 90:4

But, beloved, be not ignorant of this one thing, that one day is with the Lord as a thousand years, and a thousand years as one day. 2 Peter 3:8-9

It makes perfect sense that a loving Father in heaven would be willing to send us to an existence that would seem like an eternity to us while we pass through it, but in reality be a short time away from Him.

In fact, two- and one-half hours of God's time is approximately one hundred and four years of man's, and not many of us live to be that old. One hour of God's time takes a person to about forty-two years of age, and two hours equal about eighty-three-man years. So, my eighty-six-year-old father-in-law has only been away from heaven a little over two hours. That's hardly the length of a good movie! When you think about it that way, couldn't we do anything for two hours—couldn't we endure any trial?

When we die and return to heaven, it'll be as if we never left. At my age, I have been here, on earth, away from my true home in heaven, for only *one hour and thirteen minutes.* All I'm saying is, my room better be just the way I left it when I get back!

Death "births" us back into our true existence,
this I *know.*

This true existence is so close to us—just a thin veil away and returning there is like opening a door and stepping through it to the other side. I have great faith and hope for that, but unlike most, and for a purpose, my mortal experiences have also given me *proof.*

Faith is to hope for things not seen. Knowledge, or proof, comes from seeing or witnessing. The other-worldly experiences that I have witnessed have given me *knowledge* that something greater than what we mortally see exists.

Seventeen

We Are Not Alone

Would God create us, dump us in a dying, corruptible world, and then forget us? No! He created our spirits, lovingly placed us in magnificent bodies on a glorious, yet mortal earth, knowing that it, like us, would eventually need to be cleansed and purified before being able to abide in His presence. He gave us all the tools we need to survive, including a Savior, and the promptings of an ever-watchful friend and companion, the Holy Ghost.

About six months ago, while sitting at my computer, a clear, intense prompting came to me. I heard a thought, not of mine own, that said, *"Cleanse the inner vessel."* It's hard to explain. It wasn't like thinking about something because a particular stimulus was placed before me causing me to reflect upon it. It was much deeper, like spirit speaking to spirit. That makes sense to me, because the inner part of us is pure, eternal spirit, and the Holy Spirit is, well, a spirit—spirit, speaking to spirit. For the most part, I have continued to follow that prompting, though I still struggle.

It's interesting though because *it wasn't my thought.*

So, whose was it? It is experiences like this that cause me to testify that *there is a greater existence than that which we see* before us. We have great purpose in life—and an even greater purpose in the eternities. We are not alone—*we never have been.*

Eighteen

The Warning
Ohio, USA

Several years ago in Ohio, I had a similar spirit-to-spirit prompting. I was driving home from my dear friend, Lynn Gentry's house. I was cruising along at 55 mph on a twisting, tree-lined road, when I heard a "thought" not of mine own, say, "Slow down." I immediately listened. Now, if I had taken the time to question the thought, I wouldn't have followed it, because it made no sense. Slow down? I wasn't speeding, and there wasn't any traffic. But I didn't question it, I obeyed and slowed down to 25 mph for no apparent reason. As I rounded the bend, I came upon two disabled vehicles blocking both sides of the road. I would have been seriously injured, or worse, if I hadn't been protected by that prompting.

It wasn't my thought.

Although it was in my head, and it sounded like my voice, the way you sound to yourself when you are thinking, it was totally independent of my thought. I did not think it, nor say it, but it came from another source.

Who, I wonder? Who warned me on that dark night? Better yet why? Why was I spared, not even hurt? There are those not of this world who do watch over us and *if we listen,* they will help us through all kinds of potential calamities.

Nineteen

A Step Away

When I was a little girl growing up in the woodlands of Maine, my mom would squirt a small amount of Joy dish soap and water into a cup and give me a plastic straw. I'd take it outside our apartment in Charleston and dump a good part of it on the grass, as the ground needed a fair amount of preparation for the pointy ends of the grass not to pierce my intended creation. I'd sprawl out and rest my straw in the soap, forming an amazing array of rainbow hues atop a lush carpet of deep green.

But, as moments of joy end, I vividly remember my dismay in discovering that all bubbles die, after what appeared to be a very short life. I remember watching each iridescent bubble, with the forever-hope of a young child, that this one would not follow the same course as all the others. But alas, the empty black holes always emerged, as if tiny cancers in my bubbles—ever growing, always consuming—as is the fate of all bubbles amongst the demands of time and circumstance.

Would that I might find the secret to eternal bubbles—never dying—always remaining, but then, what would I do with them all? And who am I to assume such a lofty position? Did not each bubble fulfill their intended purpose in existing that I might have wonder and delight in their creation? And finally, would the thrill of the bubble be dimmed, if bubbles never burst, popping into frothy mists, and dissipating back into the earth?

What do I take for granted now that if it were suddenly gone, I'd mourn the loss of? What is life, if not iridescent, fragile bubbles of life and love, forever dissipating into the annals of time?

Ah, but here, I know the secret!

Life and love in all its wonder is and always will be eternal in nature and substance. It might appear to "die" as mortal does, but what waits on the other side has always existed from before the beginning of time. We return back from whence we came. This place called heaven is our true home, and it's only a step away. Per chance I might find my bubbles there?

Twenty

Deathly Sight
Spring 2009

It was probably a Saturday, because my husband and I had spent the day going from yard sale to yard sale searching for a table for our new computer. We found a beautiful chandelier instead.

We were heading west on Brown when Bill jumped and pointed forward. He had just seen the tail end of a collision at Brown and Val Vista. We were among the first at the intersection and were the first in line in the far-right lane. The cars involved in the accident came to a stop across the intersection on the other side of Val Vista—across from us, but in the east bound lanes.

Bill hopped out of our car and ran over to help along with two or three other people. I stayed in the car and watched. It didn't seem like a bad wreck from where I was sitting, and though I was concerned for the young girl behind the wheel and her friend in the back, I wasn't too worried. I watched as Bill stuck his head in the driver's side window to check on them, and then I just played the waiting game for him to return to our car so that we could get on with our busy day.

He was over there quite a while though, and after he came back, I had lots of questions. I wish I had recorded this when it happened, because too much time has elapsed for me to remember all the details. I think Bill told me that she had lost consciousness, but I'm not sure now. However, the one thing that I do remember clearly, as if it just happened yesterday, was his response when I asked him how the girl was in the back seat. He looked at me strange and said, "There wasn't anyone in the back seat—there wasn't anyone else in the car."

Yes there was. I saw her.

He was adamant about it. *He* was over there—*he* stuck his head in the car, and *he* was there for a long time, trying to help out, and I was simply sitting across the intersection, observing. I argued with him for a short while, but he would not relent, and neither would I. I truly had seen both a girl behind the wheel and another girl looking straight ahead from the back seat.

So, who did I see? I've often wondered about that—wondered if she had left her own body—and wondered why I could see her, and no one else.

Twenty-one

Walking on Water

Don't you hate it when you have a dream that shocks you awake? The other night I dreamt that Bill and I were on a narrow, well-traveled road. There were other vehicles on the road with us traveling in the same direction, but I don't remember any coming the opposite way.

We all seemed to be moving forward. We were in a terrible storm—heavy rain and wind. I didn't notice that the road we were on didn't have any side rails, until the wind and rain caused our vehicle to hydroplane off the road and onto the surface of an ocean—pocked with thousands of uniform waves—much like the surface of any water when rained upon. We skimmed the surface of the ocean for about four seconds before I assessed the situation and said, "We're going to die." I was shocked awake, and the writer/survivor in me immediately planned our escape from our impending doom.

So, I was thinking.

In my youth, I was taught the story of Peter. He looked out of his ship and saw Jesus walking on the surface of the water and desired to be with him. Christ told him to come out of the safety of the ship and walk upon the water with him, and with knowledge of the Savior right there in front of him, he took that first step, and then the second, and then the third. I remember as a child being excited to hear that story. I mean, who wouldn't like to be able to walk on the water with the Savior? Peter did and was doing just fine with his eyes and heart focused on the mark, even Jesus Christ himself, but as he felt the storm around him and looked down, he feared, and slipped into the icy water. I was not disappointed as a child with Peter's failure when the rest of the story told of how Christ stretched forth his hand and saved him. As an adult, I see a lot of similarities in my own life.

Faith.

Faith is to hope for things that you can't see.

I have great reverence for your right to believe whatever you may. For me, I believe in Christ. But even though I clearly see the mark before me, how easy it is to "look down" and slip into doubt and fear. How much this life is like walking on water while the storm rages around us! But if our focus is on the mark, we can pass through any trial. We can overcome any obstacle. We can brave any storm. Never doubt your faith, and don't look down! But if you do . . . reach up.

Twenty-two

More than a Dream
July 27, 2009

I had a pretty incredible dream on July 27, 2009. I wrote it down when I awoke. In my dream, I went outside. I was carrying something, but I don't remember what. The first thing that I noticed were the clouds. They had an unusual green tint or lining and were mounded up like columns or pillars only wide, but still topped like a cloud.

As I looked closer, I saw tiny, vertical lines at the base of the clouds, not at the bottom though, just lower than mid-point. They didn't look like part of a normal cloud, so I kept looking, and as I did, I saw that the tiny lines were a long line of people all clad in the same color as the clouds, or at least close enough to blend in. Recognizing them as angels of the Lord, I scanned across looking for the Savior, and there He was, in the center of the line. There was a slight space between Him and the angels and His arms were outstretched. I pointed to the sky and was vaguely aware that others were too but not everyone.

Those of us that saw Christ knew we were supposed to get to higher ground. Now this is where I'm fairly sure that a normal dream sequence took over.

Those of us that could see Him began to climb this mountain that appeared in front of us, while those who could not, tried to prevent us from climbing. One mother of a former student could not see the Savior, but her children could, and they came with me, but she didn't.

Now the dream begins to get strange, as dreams often do, and because those that couldn't see the Savior tried to prevent me from climbing, I was able because of my faith, to hold on to the children and simply rise in the sky.

Fascinating dream, but what does it mean? Of course, the message is clear that our example influences those whom we teach, but also there's those odd green-tinted, high-columned clouds. They were so unique, unlike any cloud I've ever seen. I will be especially observant if I ever see them again.

Twenty-three

Strange Happenings
Dover-Foxcroft, Maine, USA
USC, Los Angeles, California, USA
Batavia, Ohio, USA
Phoenix, Arizona, USA
Mesa, Arizona, USA
Circa 1974 and on
Age: 16 and up

I do not wish to record this, but I know I must, for it is as much a part of my life's experiences as the pleasant, peaceful, and joyous experiences are. I don't recall how or when they began, but I think I know where.

We moved from the dairy farm into town. My parents bought a large two-story house on Union Street. I do not have bad feelings about that house. I loved that house, even though very scary things happened within its walls. I will not elaborate or embellish with lofty words. I would much rather simply record the events and get on with it.

I saw, I felt, I heard, and I experienced the unimaginable. Stephen King hasn't written anything close to what I went through. Well, maybe he has, but my experiences were *real*, making them much more frightful than the imagined. Fourteen nights in a row, I was gripped by some unseen force, jaw locked in place, unable to move, visual, even actual electricity rippling from my head to frayed electrical cords hanging from my bedroom ceiling, a deep indentation in my leg, horrifying noises, scraping sounds as if a body was being dragged across the attic above me, and my pupils dilated to almost all black. Imagining the hand of God protecting me, and sleeping with a Bible by my side, were my only reprieve.

Later as a freshman at USC, while waiting for friends to come back to the car, I heard the horrifying sounds of wild dogs growling and gnashing their teeth. First down over the mountain, and then approaching and surrounding the car—not just beside it, but all around and above it, as if a pack of dogs were at every angle of the car, pressed tight against the glass. I couldn't see anything outside the vehicle but could only hear the terrible sounds. I prayed, and the sounds went away, but came back twice.

In Ohio, when I went downstairs into Bill's parent's family room, I saw a plant on a pedestal rocking rhythmically back and forth. And one evening, I saw just the head of a very frightening apparition, in full horrific color, floating above me while I lay on my bed. In all of the horror movies, or television shows depicting such things, I have never seen anything so wicked—the expression on his face was evil beyond imagination. But he couldn't hurt nor harm me in any way— only frighten me and cause me to seek more answers.

Spirits? Two that were alarming, one that was not, with her long gray hair, and quiet demeanor. One who was a young girl about ten or twelve, I've seen her at least three times in different locations, once with a young boy, dark hair, slightly older than she. And then of course, seeing my deceased father standing at the foot of my bed and hearing the reassuring voice of my deceased brother.

Why me? Why not everyone?

Maybe I needed to experience the evil to appreciate the good. Maybe I've been chosen to stand as a witness that these things exist. Maybe I can help someone realize that they need not fear the unknown, for that is what I have learned.

Or maybe, I was meant to understand the spirit world, so I could *write* about it. Authors often build worlds from study and experience, and though the angels and demons in my *No Angel* series are fictional, they are based on as much truth as I could glean from books and personal experience.

Epilogue

Though I have had proof that spirits, demons, and angels exist, my faith in Jesus Christ supersedes knowledge. I believe in Jesus Christ, and yet I have not seen Him.

There is more to life than meets the eye.

One must make it their own personal mission to search for truth and equally important—accept it and live it.

Truth is—

The life after death that we all wonder about *is what we ought to be focused on while here in mortality*—our choices here determine our eternal destiny.

In an effort to turn us away from focusing on our truer existence and our inevitable return to it, Satan seeks to take our focus away from *who we are*, literal children of a loving Father in Heaven; *why we are here* in mortality, to prove ourselves worthy to obtain all that our Father has in store for us; and *where we will go* after mortality, back to our heavenly home on high, either triumphantly, or damned—dependent upon our earthly choices.

Satan seeks to destroy us and would have us forget who

we are, but God destines us to eternity and would have us live our lives preparing for it.

 Author Theresa Sneed graduated cum laude with a BA in education. Though retired as a fulltime teacher, she enjoys visiting classrooms and sharing her writing journey. Her books are unique; each story takes you places you've never imagined before. She writes across six genres: mystery and suspense, fantasy, historical fiction/time-travel, realistic paranormal, nonfiction motivational, and children's books. All of Theresa's fiction books have elements of sweet romance, and while none of her books have profanity or sexually explicit scenes, each book is intriguing and white-knuckle intense—the kind you can't put down.

Her nonfiction books are *So You Want to Write: A Guide to Writing Your First Book* where Theresa has pulled together her fifteen steps to writing success; *Fantastic Covers and How to Make Them*; and *Facing Mortality: Dreams & Other Significant Things* a compilation of Theresa's paranormal experiences that drove her to write her *No Angel* series and many scenes in her other works.

Theresa's first picture book explores the woes of sibling tattletales. *Brown Nose Bear* is a children's story that kept her own children and now her grandchildren giggling and rethinking whether tattletales should or should not be told.

The *No Angel* series is the story about a guardian angel with an attitude, and the ever present, but misunderstood spirit world. There are five published books in the series with many more to come. Book one, formerly called *No Angel*, is now called *Angel with an Attitude*; book two, formerly called

Earthbound, is now called *Earthbound Angel*; book three is called *Destiny's Angel*; book four is called *Earth Angel,* and book five is called *Harold Angel Sing.*

With the addition of *Missing Medallion,* The *Sons of Elderberry* series has three books, books one and two called *Elias of Elderberry* and *The Wood Fairies of Estraelia.* Harry-Potterish with wizards, fairies, elves, pixies, yōkai shapeshifters, and dragons, this story has it all! Theresa anticipates another book or two to finish this series.

Escape is the story of a fifteen-year-old girl abducted by a corrupt sheriff in the 70's. He keeps her captive in his cellar for five years, until she escapes with his truck and his young daughter. *Escape* is book one in the *Escape* series. Book two is *You Can't Hide,* and book three, *Find Her Keep Her,* ends the gripping saga.

As the ninth great-granddaughter of one of the women hanged as a witch in Salem, Theresa Sneed has a vested interest in telling her story as accurately as possible. She wrote the *Salem Witch Haunt* series to be a voice for her grandmother. Thoroughly researched, all interactions with real people from that era are based on primary sources. In book one, *Salem Witch Haunt,* the trial scene with Theresa's 9th great-grandmother, Susannah Martin is taken from Reverend Samuel Parris's handwritten transcript verbatim. *Salem Witch Haunt* was intended to be a standalone book, until the shocking ending made it apparent that the characters were not finished telling their story. Hence, *Return to Salem,* where the second set of trials and hangings in Salem, 1692, are masterfully woven into the story. *Salem Bewitched* completes this series with the last of the trials and hangings and the peine forte et dure of Giles Corey. Added to this series comes, *Salem Witch Haunt: Stranger Than Fiction,* where footnotes pointing to the primary sources embedded in the series have been added as a companion to this incredible historical fiction. Both *Return to Salem: Stranger Than Fiction* and *Salem Bewitched: Stranger Than Fiction* will come later.

Learn more about Theresa's books at www.theresasneed.com. She loves hearing from her readers and may be contacted through her website or through her email at tmsneed@theresasneed.com Stay connected with new releases and free eBook offers by signing up at her website.